SURRENDERED

YIELDING TO GOD'S PERFECT WILL

30 Day Devotional

Nate Stevens

Copyright © 2023 by Nate Stevens

All rights reserved. No part of this publication may be reproduced, distributed, or transmitted in any form or by any means, including photocopying, recording, or other electronic or mechanical methods, without the prior written permission of the publisher, except in the case of brief quotations embodied in critical reviews and certain other noncommercial uses permitted by copyright law. For permission requests, please write to the publisher at publishing@kingdomwinds.com.

Unless otherwise indicated, Scripture quotations are from The New King James Version (NKJV) / Thomas Nelson Publishers, Nashville: Thomas Nelson Publishers. Copyright © 1982. Used by permission. All rights reserved.

Scripture quotations marked (KJV) are taken from the King James Version. Public Domain.

Scripture quotations marked (NLT) are taken from the Holy Bible, New Living Translation, copyright © 1996, 2004, 2015 by Tyndale House Foundation. Used by permission of Tyndale House Publishers, a Division of Tyndale House Ministries, Carol Stream, Illinois 60188. All rights reserved.

Scripture quotations marked (TLB) are taken from The Living Bible Copyright © 1971 by Tyndale House Foundation. Used by permission of Tyndale House Publishers Inc., Carol Stream, Illinois 60188. All rights reserved.

First Edition, 2023
ISBN: 978-1-64590-043-6

Published by Kingdom Winds Publishing.
6 Charleston Oak Lane, Greenville, SC 29615
www.kingdomwinds.com
publishing@kingdomwinds.com
Printed in the United States of America.

Cover Design by Christine Dupre

The views expressed in this book are not necessarily those of the publisher.

ACKNOWLEDGEMENT

First and foremost, thank you, Jesus Christ, Lord and Savior, for demonstrating a life of obedience and surrender. With Your eternal Spirit and everlasting Word as our guides, help us live in obedience and surrender to You. May we yield every thought, action, desire, and decision to Your perfect will. May we honor You in all we say, think, and do.

Additionally, thank you, Karen Stevens, for your faithful patience and assistance in choosing which devotions to include as well as helping develop the cover concept. Along with my heart, you have my gratitude. I love you!

Finally, thank you, Gary and Elizabeth Suess and the Kingdom Winds family for your partnership in this endeavor. I am grateful for your vision and ministry to support authors, songwriters, artists, and others as they fulfill their roles in building and equipping the eternal Kingdom of God. Bless you!

ENDORSEMENT

My friend, Nate Stevens, has a rare gift for communicating powerful biblical principles through his writing in a way that is both easy to understand and captivating. His latest work, *Surrendered*, is no exception. This 30-day devotion speaks directly to the hearts of believers and seekers alike and is a natural continuation of his previous works *Transformed*, *Conformed*, and *Informed*.

As a bestselling author of numerous books on the US military, but more importantly, as a lover of God's word as perfectly given to us through the divine revelation of the Holy Scriptures, I highly recommend *Surrendered* as a must-read. It's perfect for personal enjoyment, daily quiet time, or as a supplement to Bible study. Nate Stevens is a great writer, and *Surrendered* is a powerful addition to any spiritual journey.

Don Brown

Author of National Bestsellers *Last Fighter Pilot* (2017), *Treason* (2009), and *Malacca Conspiracy* (2010), as well as 15 books on the US Military.

www.donbrownbooks.com

INTRODUCTION

Every person is as surrendered to God as he or she chooses to be. Relinquishing, the initial step of surrender, is the letting go of personal claims and desires. However, complete surrender involves the personal acknowledgement of God's rightful claim on everything—His undisputed occupancy in, and possession of, our hearts and lives. Surrender is our full acceptance of whatever God plans—no matter the pain, cost, circumstances, or outcome.

Yielding ourselves, our desires, and our lives to God may initially seem scary. But it is not something to fear or avoid due to its unknown outcome, uncertain personal impact, or perceived lack of control. Knowing that God is all-knowing, sovereign, and loving, we can trust Him fully.

Surrendering is the opposite of struggling. If we're struggling, the inner war still rages. Self still competes for the throne of life. Selfish desires, preferential passions, even unyielded ambitions are signs of struggling. On the other hand, surrender means the war is over. That happens when Self raises the flag of truce and fully yields the throne to God.

As we increasingly yield, there is an ongoing commitment of listening to the Master—reading His Word, hearing His Spirit—then obeying and applying it to our lives. It is immediately going when He says, "Go," stopping what He says to "Lay aside" or "Put off," and doing precisely and fully what He says. And we do all this without arguing, resisting, ignoring, inserting ourselves into the conversation, or negotiating our level of involvement. The supreme prayer of full surrender is, "Not my will, Father, but Yours be done."

Surrender is immediate and humble obedience to what God says, when He says it, with a loving heart—then anticipating His next assignment. We do this not to earn His favor but because He has already enveloped us in it. A true follower pleases his Master to hear Him say, "Well done, good and faithful servant!" (Matthew 25:23).

These concise daily devotions encourage such a surrendered mindset. May they be daily echoes of Jesus's call to follow and obey Him. More than just reading them daily, I encourage you to meditate on them. Apply them to your life. Allow them to kindle a deeper desire to surrender, obedience, and closer intimacy with God.

Above all else, may this 30-day journey encourage you to willingly and gratefully surrender to God's "good and acceptable and perfect will" (Romans 12:2).

Nate Stevens

SURRENDERED TO GOD – DAY 1

Keeping Your Temple Holy
(1 Corinthians 6:19–20)

In the Old Testament, priests zealously guarded the Temple against any and all impurity and defilement. They protected the sphere of holiness. When idolatry crept into the Temple, God's glory and presence departed (Ezekiel 10). Genuine Christians are the temples of God's Holy Spirit. God, through His Holy Spirit, dwells within us (John 14:17). Just as God's presence came to dwell in the protected, holy Temple, we are to be pure, consecrated, and holy temples (1 Peter 1:15–16). To maintain the vibrant presence and power of God, we must protect our sphere of holiness from even the slightest impurity. God will not share His glory with anything or anyone (Isaiah 48:11)—especially any tolerated impurity.

Loving Father, please search my heart. Show me any impurity that hinders Your active presence and power in my life. I yield it to You even now.

SURRENDERED TO GOD – JOURNAL DAY 1

What tolerated or "excused" impurity remains in my life today? How will I protect my sphere of holiness?

_____

_____

_____

_____

_____

_____

_____

_____

_____

SURRENDERED TO GOD – DAY 2

Cattle Trail or Highway?
(Jeremiah 18:15)

"Because My people have forgotten Me…they have caused themselves to…walk in pathways and not on a highway." Growing up on a farm, I became familiar with the well-worn trails made by our cows. Cattle trails are narrow, uneven, and slow-paced. Quite the opposite, highways are wide, level, and intended for speed. Following God's purpose, will, and Word makes for smoother, more efficient, and more successful journeys (Isaiah 40:3). Straying onto cattle trails involves rough, agonizing, and regrettable rides (Proverbs 13:15). We may choose either option, but the consequences are not optional. The Prodigal Son (Luke 15:11–24) chose to rough it but soon desired the open road back home to his father.

Father God, keep me on Your pathway so nothing causes me to stumble (Psalm 119:165).

SURRENDERED TO GOD – JOURNAL DAY 2

As I surrender to God in all areas of life, which cattle trail will I exchange for God's highway?

_____

_____

_____

_____

_____

_____

_____

_____

_____

SURRENDERED TO GOD – DAY 3

The Master-Servant Relationship
(Luke 6:40)

Several New Testament writers identified themselves as "bondservants" of God (Paul, James, Peter, Jude). The Greek word used implies voluntary submission or service. In a master-servant relationship, the master talks, directs, and decides; the servant listens and obeys. There is no hesitation or negotiation, simply obedience to the master's heart. With Christ as Savior, we accept Christ's eternal salvation. With Christ as Lord, we surrender and obey Him immediately. We are willingly His servants, to perform what He asks, without delay and with grateful, loving, and reverent hearts. No assignment is too small, no request too large. When we stand before Him one day, may we hear Him say, "Well done, good and faithful servant" (Matthew 25:23).

Heavenly Father, You are my Savior and Lord. Thank You for saving me eternally. Help and empower me to follow and obey You faithfully!

Yielding to God's Perfect Will

SURRENDERED TO GOD – JOURNAL DAY 3

How am I a "bondservant" of God? In what area(s) am I still hesitating and/or negotiating?

_____
_____
_____
_____
_____
_____
_____
_____
_____

SURRENDERED TO GOD – DAY 4

God Reveals the Journey When We Take the Steps Already Shown (Psalm 119:105)

God's word is "a lamp to my feet and a light to my path." *Lamp* refers to a burning candle that lights a small portion of a pathway. It yields just enough light for the immediate steps ahead. However, *light* describes illumination in every sense, including brightening something as radiantly as when it is in direct sunlight. It implies enlightening or revealing the entire journey. Trusting God involves taking steps of obedience in what we already know before asking His direction about the unknown. Obey today and trust God for further light for tomorrow.

Father, help me to walk each day in the light You give—the truth, morals, and standards of Your Word—and trust You to illuminate the journey ahead.

Yielding to God's Perfect Will

SURRENDERED TO GOD – JOURNAL DAY 4

What has God already shown me to do in obedience to His Word? What steps am I taking to obey?

_____

_____

_____

_____

_____

_____

_____

_____

_____

SURRENDERED TO GOD – DAY 5

Love Affects Surrender (2 John 1:6)

"This is love, that we walk according to His commandments." The mind stipulates an "I ought to" mindset. The will mandates an "I have to" mindset. But the heart compels an "I love to" mindset and lifestyle. Hiding God's Word in our hearts (Psalm 119:11) creates an urgency to obey Him—not because we ought to or have to but because we want to, we desire to, we long to. We want to please our Savior and Lord—the One who gave His life because He loves us. Jesus said, "If you love Me, keep My commandments" (John 14:15). When Jesus lives at the center of my heart and remains enthroned there, I am drawn to my Beloved. It is in the heart where holiness takes root. The heart is where commitment and surrender reside. Where logic and willpower fail, love prevails.

Loving Heavenly Father, thank You for loving me unconditionally. My heart longs to obey You.

Yielding to God's Perfect Will

SURRENDERED TO GOD - JOURNAL DAY 5

How does God's amazing, overwhelming love for me influence my surrender and obedience to Him?

_____
_____
_____
_____
_____
_____
_____
_____
_____

SURRENDERED TO GOD – DAY 6

*The Inadequacy of Surrender
(2 Corinthians 12:10, TLB)*

"When I am weak, then I am strong—the less I have, the more I depend on Him." Most of the people God used mightily experienced an acute sense of inadequacy. Moses struggled with his stammering tongue. Isaiah cried, "Woe *is* me, for I am undone!" (Isaiah 6:5). Gideon perceived himself insignificant to the task. Jeremiah struggled with his youth and inexperience. When we feel inadequate or unqualified for whatever task God offers, He welcomes our surrender and strengthens our weakness with His power. By feeling qualified and self-sufficient, we operate in our own strength (and fail), and God receives no glory. He reserves His power for those who desperately need Him, rely fully on Him, and surrender to Him all honor for the outcome.

Holy Father, help me do everything in complete dependence on You.

SURRENDERED TO GOD – JOURNAL DAY 6

What must I relinquish to live the Christian life through the power of Christ (Galatians 2:20)?

_____

_____

_____

_____

_____

_____

_____

_____

_____

SURRENDERED TO GOD – DAY 7

*Leading Others in Obedience to God
(Genesis 31:16)*

"Now then, whatever God has said to you, do it." As Jacob prepared his large family to leave Laban, he shared the dream God gave him about their departure. For years, his father-in-law consistently deceived Jacob and changed his wages ten times (Genesis 31:7). But God blessed Jacob despite such treachery. Laban's daughters saw their father's mistreatment and agreed to follow Jacob as God instructed. Leaving family and employment, compounded by unresolved family conflict, was an extremely difficult decision. Yet surrender and obedience to God always take top priority—and receive His blessing and favor.

Loving Father, when, where, and how You lead is always in my best interest and deserves my immediate submission. Following You and leading others in obedience is my responsibility before You—one I do not take lightly.

Yielding to God's Perfect Will

SURRENDERED TO GOD - JOURNAL DAY 7

Who may be following my example today? How can I encourage others to walk in obedience with God?

_____

_____

_____

_____

_____

_____

_____

_____

SURRENDERED TO GOD – DAY 8

Obedience Invites God's Favor and Presence
(Exodus 39:43)

"As the LORD had commanded, just so they had done it." Upon the Tabernacle's completion, with all the specific materials and sacred contents required, Moses inspected the work. Even with the tedious instructions, measurements, and minute details, they fulfilled all specifications as God had instructed. And the result was spectacular. As a result, the glorious presence of the LORD God Almighty descended and filled the Tabernacle (Exodus 40:35). The same happens when God's people obey His instructions in life, lifestyle, and witness. Obedience brings God's favor and blessings along with His intimate presence. Disobeying or disregarding Him results in His discipline, disfavor, and silence.

Father God, no matter how seemingly insignificant a particular life issue may be, may I always seek Your guidance and surrender to Your instruction and will.

Yielding to God's Perfect Will

SURRENDERED TO GOD – JOURNAL DAY 8

What unsurrendered area is restricting God's favor, blessings, and intimate presence in my life?

_____

_____

_____

_____

_____

_____

_____

_____

_____

_____

SURRENDERED TO GOD – DAY 9

Obedient to the Point of Death
(Philippians 2:8)

Jesus "humbled Himself and became obedient *to the point of* death." Obedience involves a certain level of humility. However, obedience to the point of death is the dedication to fulfill an assigned task regardless of personal cost. Partial obedience is an oxymoron that signals disregard and disobedience. In following Christ's example, we resolve ourselves to complete obedience, even at the expense of life itself. "For consider Him who endured such hostility from sinners against Himself, lest you become weary and discouraged in your souls. You have not yet resisted to bloodshed, striving against sin" (Hebrews 12:3–4). Faith and love for God is measured by the extent to which we obey Him and His moral standard (John 14:15).

Father God, seal and steel my heart and mind in obedience to You. I am Yours, come what may.

Yielding to God's Perfect Will

SURRENDERED TO GOD - JOURNAL DAY 9

What steps am I taking on the journey of holiness? How have I surrendered my life to God?

_____

_____

_____

_____

_____

_____

_____

_____

_____

SURRENDERED TO GOD – DAY 10

Disobedience Affects Others (1 Samuel 30)

God told Saul to annihilate the wicked Amalekites. However, Saul disobeyed and left many alive (1 Samuel 15:1–9). Years later, these same people invaded David's city, capturing all he had and taking his family hostage. Ultimately, David fought back, defeated them, and recovered everything. However, this misfortune would never have happened if Saul had obeyed God from the start. Disobedience to God's moral law and direction always has consequences. God rejected Saul as king, and Saul later paid for his disobedience with his life (1 Samuel 31). May we be fully obedient to please our Lord and avoid the rippling consequences of disobedience.

Heavenly Father, my heart's desire is to immediately and fully obey You. Instead of causing rippling effects of disobedience or doubt, may I be a channel of Your blessings for those in my areas of influence.

Yielding to God's Perfect Will

SURRENDERED TO GOD - JOURNAL DAY 10

How has my past disobedience affected others in my life? How have I grown spiritually since then?

_____

_____

_____

_____

_____

_____

_____

_____

_____

SURRENDERED TO GOD - DAY 11

God's Conditional Blessing
(Joshua 23:10–11)

"The LORD your God is He who fights for you, as He promised you. Therefore, take careful heed...that you love the LORD your God." In Joshua's farewell speech, he reminded the Israelites of God's many blessings—spanning their Exodus from Egyptian bondage to their victories in the Promised Land. He confirmed it was God who delivered their enemies into their hands. But he also warned, should they forsake God and turn to the foreign gods of the surrounding pagan nations, God would no longer fight on their behalf. Rather, He would withhold His protective assistance and allow their destruction. God is holy and jealous (Joshua 24:19). He cannot tolerate sin, nor will He bless even partial obedience.

Father, from today forward, I choose to surrender, faithfully follow, and intentionally obey You.

SURRENDERED TO GOD – JOURNAL DAY 11

How has God disciplined me for disobeying Him and/or rewarded me for obeying Him?

_____
_____
_____
_____
_____
_____
_____
_____
_____

SURRENDERED TO GOD - DAY 12

Walk Worthy (Colossians 1:10)

God calls His followers to "walk worthy of the Lord, fully pleasing Him, being fruitful in every good work and increasing in the knowledge of God." This walking worthily involves God-honoring daily conduct and lifestyles (Ephesians 4:1). We walk worthy of God who calls us to His kingdom and glory (1 Thessalonians 2:12), not to earn our way, but to please Him who has called us to Himself (2 Timothy 2:4). As God's children, spiritually reborn, we bear the family resemblance and are His ambassadors to the unbelieving world. This "worthy walk" confirms our dedicated passion for God while shining His light to unbelievers. May our walk of a lifetime be worthy of God's eternal rewards when He tests it with His refining fire (1 Corinthians 3:12–15).

Holy Spirit, fill me and guide me to walk worthy before Father God in all I think, say, and do.

SURRENDERED TO GOD – JOURNAL DAY 12

How does my daily walk align with God's Word? How am I walking "worthy of the Lord"?

_____

_____

_____

_____

_____

_____

_____

_____

_____

SURRENDERED TO GOD – DAY 13

Even the Seemingly Senseless and Illogical
(Jeremiah 13:1–7)

Do we obey God even when what He asks seems pointless or confusing? Jeremiah faced this question when God asked him to buy a new linen sash then bury it. Many days later when God asked him to dig it up, he found it ruined and worthless. So why give this puzzling request? Why not simply ask Jeremiah to use one of his old, worthless garments? That is the essence of obedience: immediate, unquestioned action even when facing apparent futility. Along with obedience, implicit trust in the Requestor produces unconditional submission. As Abraham demonstrated on Mt. Moriah, there can be no negotiation, only acceptance. No discussion, only agreement. No substitution, only surrender.

Father God, help me to surrender to You without negotiation, discussion, or reservation.

Yielding to God's Perfect Will

SURRENDERED TO GOD – JOURNAL DAY 13

What seemingly confusing, illogical, or difficult thing is God asking of me? How will I respond?

_____

_____

_____

_____

_____

_____

_____

_____

_____

SURRENDERED TO GOD – DAY 14

The Sound of God's Footsteps (Genesis 3:8)

"And they heard the sound of the LORD God walking in the garden in the cool of the day." What do God's footsteps sound like? Adam and Eve recognized that sound when He came looking for them after their sin in the Garden of Eden. When we disobey His moral standard, the sound of His approach is most terrifying. Just like Adam and Eve, we often try to hide ourselves from God as the shame, guilt, and regret of sin overwhelm us. However, when we walk in obedience to Him, His steps sound comforting like the familiar, confident stride of a loving parent or lifelong friend. May we live in such a way that we anticipate and welcome the sound of God's footsteps.

Loving Father, thank You for continuing to come looking for me. Your approaching sound reassures me of Your love.

SURRENDERED TO GOD - JOURNAL DAY 14

How comfortable am I in God's intimate presence? What does the sound of His footsteps mean to me?

_____

_____

_____

_____

_____

_____

_____

_____

_____

SURRENDERED TO GOD – DAY 15

Crucified with Christ (Galatians 5:24)

"Those *who are* Christ's have crucified the flesh with its passions and desires." Followers of Christ maintain the free will to choose their behaviors and actions. The submissive act of taking up Christ's cross daily involves dying to self, including all worldly affections and forbidden cravings. To do so, we relinquish and extinguish anything contrary to God's Word and the Spirit's guidance. Something crucified is dying yet may still struggle for life. Our sinful nature still craves carnal affections, sinful influences, and worldly desires. We resolve the conflict between the sinful and spiritual natures by reminding ourselves, "I have been crucified with Christ; it is no longer I who live, but Christ lives in me" (Galatians 2:20a).

Holy Father, forgive me and keep me from the slightest sinful tolerance that breathes life into what has been crucified with You. I yield it to You.

Yielding to God's Perfect Will

SURRENDERED TO GOD – JOURNAL DAY 15

What carnal passion or worldly desire am I battling? Am I willing to surrender it to God and die to it?

_____

_____

_____

_____

_____

_____

_____

_____

_____

SURRENDERED TO GOD – DAY 16

*Release Past Blessings to Receive the New
(Leviticus 26:10)*

"You shall eat the old harvest, and clear out the old because of the new." Though grateful for every blessing, we are called to move on from past favor in anticipation of God's new. His mercy, compassion, and faithfulness are renewed every morning (Lamentations 3:22–23). He promises to do a new thing (Isaiah 43:19). Jesus invites us to lift up our heads, get a new perspective, and anticipate the new thing He is doing (John 4:35). Paul encourages a lifestyle of newness of life (Romans 6:4). But God's blessing is contingent on the "if" of our obedience: "If you walk in My statutes and keep My commandments, and perform them, then I will give …" (Leviticus 26:3–4).

Father, I surrender every aspect of my life to You and choose to live in anticipation of Your new.

Yielding to God's Perfect Will

SURRENDERED TO GOD - JOURNAL DAY 16

How has God blessed my past obedience? What "new thing" of surrender is He presenting to me?

_____

_____

_____

_____

_____

_____

_____

_____

_____

SURRENDERED TO GOD – DAY 17

Avoiding God's Rejection (Numbers 14:34)

"You shall know My rejection." The Israelites wandered in the wilderness for forty years—one year for each day they spied out the Promised Land. When the twelve men returned, ten gave an intimidating report about ferocious, gigantic inhabitants and monstrous, well-fortified cities. Only Joshua and Caleb remained faithful to God, trusting His promise to help them overcome all obstacles and possess the land. God asked Moses, "How long will these people reject Me? And how long will they not believe Me…?" (Numbers 14:11). Instead of whimsically overlooking their unbelief and rebellion, God prohibited them from the Promised Land and returned them to the wilderness where an entire generation died as a result of their unbelief (Numbers 14:33). It is far better to believe, trust, and obey God.

Oh, God, help me to always trust, rely on, and immediately obey You and Your Word.

SURRENDERED TO GOD - JOURNAL DAY 17

How am I avoiding God's rejection? In what area(s) am I still doubting Him or resisting His influence?

_____
_____
_____
_____
_____
_____
_____
_____

SURRENDERED TO GOD – DAY 18

Self-denial Versus Self-death (Colossians 2:23)

"An appearance of wisdom in self-imposed religion…" A counterfeit perception exists in a works-based religion. Situational humility and occasional self-denial may appear as sacred acts deserving our participation. Yet they provide no lasting value against the pampering of our carnal nature. Any religion or religious observance—yes, even spiritual service or ministry—dependent on what we can do in our own strength wields no power against fleshly desires. Instead of mere self-denial, God calls us to self-death, to crucify our affections and desires, and keep ourselves "unspotted" from the world (James 1:27). We can override self-denial when desires become passionate enough. But self-death is the complete surrender to the Holy Spirit's influence and the willingness to obey God's Word.

Father, I willingly die daily so Your Spirit, Your Word, and Your way may actively influence me.

SURRENDERED TO GOD – JOURNAL DAY 18

Have I surrendered my Christian service or ministry to God? How am I "dying and denying" daily?

_____
_____
_____
_____
_____
_____
_____
_____
_____

SURRENDERED TO GOD – DAY 19

God Blesses, But Also Curses
(Deuteronomy 28:15, 28)

"If you do not obey the voice of the LORD your God...the LORD will strike you with madness and blindness and confusion of heart." Disobeying God usually results in His removing His blessings and protection from our lives. In that disciplined state, we think irrationally, discern inaccurately, and are easily deceived. Mental confusion, blindness, and anxiety are our new norms. Nebuchadnezzar learned this the hard way when God judged his arrogance with a seven-year mental nightmare (Daniel 4). Yes, God is loving, patient, and compassionate; but He is also immutably holy, fiercely jealous, and loves us too much to allow our disobedience without disciplining us.

Loving Father, thank You for Your unchangeable standard, unconditional love, and purifying discipline. Grant me clarity, discernment, and favor as I obey and surrender to You.

SURRENDERED TO GOD – JOURNAL DAY 19

How does my love for God affect my obedience and surrender to Him? What does my resistance reveal?

_____
_____
_____
_____
_____
_____
_____
_____
_____
_____

SURRENDERED TO GOD – DAY 20

Use Your Resources Wisely (Isaiah 55:2)

"Why do you spend money for *what is* not bread, and your wages for *what* does not satisfy?" Inside the human heart resides an innate and insatiable hunger. We try to fill that unknown craving with many things, all of which eventually dissatisfy. Jesus confirmed, "Man shall not live by bread alone, but by every word that proceeds from the mouth of God" (Matthew 4:4). God alone satisfies the hunger deep within. The sooner we accept and incorporate that truth into our lives, the sooner we will be filled (Matthew 5:6). In addition, we will all give account before God for what He entrusted to us (Matthew 25:14–30). May we be conscientious and wise when spending the time, gifts, talents, and resources God gives us.

Heavenly Father, remove from me anyone and anything that could become an idol or distraction from You and Your Word. I yield my all to You.

SURRENDERED TO GOD – JOURNAL DAY 20

What or who still dominates my heart? What prevents me from surrendering it all to God?

_____

_____

_____

_____

_____

_____

_____

_____

_____

_____

SURRENDERED TO GOD – DAY 21

"Do You Love Me?" (John 21:15–17)

After His resurrection, when Jesus asked Peter if he loved Him, it was a confirmation for Peter, not a condemnation from Jesus. Being omniscient, Jesus already knew the condition of Peter's heart and the level of love he had for his Lord. After his conversion and indwelling by the Holy Spirit at Pentecost, Peter boldly preached Jesus as Savior and Lord (Acts 2:14–36). Before being executed for his faith, he wrote, "Love will cover a multitude of sins" (1 Peter 4:8). What else but God's love and forgiveness could command such boldness and commitment? Jesus confirmed our level of love coincides with our recognition of forgiveness—much forgiveness provokes much love (Luke 7:47). Do we love much?

Dear God, Your great love for me motivates my full surrender to You. Align my heart with Yours, and may my life please and glorify You.

SURRENDERED TO GOD – JOURNAL DAY 21

How does knowing God has forgiven me so much affect my love for and obedience to Him?

_____

_____

_____

_____

_____

_____

_____

_____

_____

_____

SURRENDERED TO GOD - DAY 22

Placing Past Wounds in God's Hands
(Psalm 139:23–24, NLT)

"Search me, O God, and know my heart; test me and know my anxious thoughts. Point out anything in me that offends you." When broken bones heal incorrectly, a doctor must re-break and reset them for full healing to occur. In resetting our emotional breaks and wounds, God may ask us to relinquish remaining traces of bitterness or anger toward disloyal friends. He may prompt forgiveness for ex-spouses who abandoned or abused us. He may encourage us to pray for those who have broken or betrayed our hearts. He may ask that we bless those who speak against us. Through it all, we surrender to His ongoing transformation of us into Christlikeness.

Father God, whatever You bring to mind, help me respond and resolve it quickly. I yield it to You fully as this is the quickest path to healing, wholeness, and freedom from past hurts.

Yielding to God's Perfect Will

SURRENDERED TO GOD - JOURNAL DAY 22

Have I given God full access to every corner of my heart? What "pain" remains unsurrendered to Him?

SURRENDERED TO GOD - DAY 23

*Partial Obedience = Future Struggles
(Judges 1 and 2)*

"You have not obeyed My voice. Why have you done this? Therefore...they shall be *thorns* in your side, and their gods shall be a snare to you" (Judges 2:2–3). God instructed the Israelites to remove all traces of pagan worship from the Promised Land. However, they disobeyed, not only tolerating the worship of false gods but also participating in it. So, God disciplined them by allowing their enemies to invade and defeat them. "Wherever they went out, the hand of the LORD was against them for calamity" (Judges 2:15). God's favor in this life directly coincides with surrender and obedience to Him. May we reduce unnecessary struggles and hardships by quickly and consistently obeying Him.

Loving Father, You instruct us to avoid and remove what is sinful. May I be wise enough to listen and courageous enough to obey You immediately.

SURRENDERED TO GOD – JOURNAL DAY 23

What effects of past disobedience motivate me to obey God's Word and surrender everything to Him?

_____

_____

_____

_____

_____

_____

_____

_____

_____

_____

SURRENDERED TO GOD - DAY 24

Prioritizing God's Will and Affection
(Matthew 10:37)

By saying that anyone "who loves [their family members] more than Me is not worthy of Me," it seems Jesus devalued the love of family below love for Him. On the contrary, He accentuated not only familial love, He also confirmed how much deeper our love for Him should be. Yet not only our love, but so also should our commitment and surrender to Him be. If He is not Lord over all, He is not Lord at all. There is no partial Lordship. Even a small glimpse of all He sacrificed and endured on Calvary for us should motivate us to enthrone Him as first priority. How can we thank Him for saving us eternally yet deny Him complete Lordship through disobedience and unwillingness to surrender to His will?

Heavenly Father, guide my steps according to Your will and purpose. I claim you as my Savior; I crown You as Lord of my life. Use me as You see fit.

SURRENDERED TO GOD – JOURNAL DAY 24

What priority is usurping God's rightful place in my life? What steps will I take to make Him Lord of all?

_____

_____

_____

_____

_____

_____

_____

_____

_____

SURRENDERED TO GOD - DAY 25

Time to Get Moving (Deuteronomy 1:6-7)

"You have dwelt long enough at this mountain. Turn and take your journey ..." Although God is longsuffering with our delays or hesitations, there comes a time when He prompts us into action. The Israelites had camped around Mount Sinai for about a year. While there, they watched God reveal Himself through fire, smoke, and rumbling ground. It was there He gave His Law as preparation for life in the Promised Land. But He did not want them staying at Mt. Sinai forever. He wanted them to leave and fulfill the purpose awaiting them elsewhere. Just as Jesus told the disabled man, "Take up your bed and walk" (John 5:8), God calls us to action. May we follow immediately, surrender completely, and obey fully.

Heavenly Father, after spending time in Your glorious presence and hearing Your specific direction, prompt me into action.

SURRENDERED TO GOD – JOURNAL DAY 25

How passionately do I incorporate what God reveals? How does obedience affect my intimacy with Him?

SURRENDERED TO GOD – DAY 26

The Capacity to Obey God
(Deuteronomy 32:47)

God's Word "is not a futile thing for you, because it is your life." In his final words before dying, Moses encouraged the Israelites to "Set your hearts on all the words ..." he had shared as direct instructions from God (Deuteronomy 32:46). After his death, it would be their choice to obey and follow—but it was all possible. They had the capacity to obey because God never asks anyone anything he or she cannot do. What He asks, He enables by His blood, Word, and Spirit. Obeying Him and surrendering to His will are not impossible or hopelessly ideal endeavors. They are the keys to God's favor and blessing in this world and eternal rewards in the world to come.

Father God, You have "set before [me] life and death, blessing and cursing"—I choose life and Your blessing (Deuteronomy 30:19).

SURRENDERED TO GOD – JOURNAL DAY 26

In what area(s) am I struggling to fully surrender to God? What is causing my resistance?

_____

_____

_____

_____

_____

_____

_____

_____

_____

SURRENDERED TO GOD - DAY 27

Follow Christ by Listening, Not by Seeing
(2 Corinthians 5:7)

"We walk by faith, not by sight." Jesus said His sheep, His followers, *hear* His voice and then follow Him (John 10:27). They follow because they *hear* Him, not because they necessarily *see* Him. Following only what we hear requires a considerable amount of faith and awareness. But "faith comes by hearing, and hearing [comes] by the Word of God (Romans 10:17). We increase our faith, not by seeing Him or experiencing what He does for us, but by hearing Him through His Word and His Spirit. We read. He speaks; we listen. He leads; we follow. This increases our faith and demonstrates our obedience—even when we do not fully know all the events, circumstances, and outcomes involved.

Father, along with praying, "Lord, increase [my] faith" (Luke 17:5) and "Help my unbelief" (Mark 9:24), prompt me to spend quality time with You then listen, trust, and follow.

SURRENDERED TO GOD - JOURNAL DAY 27

What is God showing me in my quiet time with Him and His Word? How am I applying it in my life?

_____

_____

_____

_____

_____

_____

_____

_____

_____

SURRENDERED TO GOD – DAY 28

Obedience to God is Like Music (Psalm 96:1)

"Sing to the LORD a new song!" I have loved Gospel music since childhood. On Saturday nights, I enjoyed listening as mom practiced (on piano and organ) the songs she would play in church on Sunday. Most of the songs, both lyrics and music, remain with me today. Music is very precise—each note specifically written to create a harmonious sound. God's Word and moral standard are similarly precise. Obedience to His instruction yields a life in harmony with Him and others. We are free to obey or disobey Him just as we may choose to sing in tune or off key. No matter how loudly or forcefully we sing the wrong notes, we only produce disharmony. But, oh, the harmonious anthem when hearts and lives are tuned to God. May we praise Him with obedience and surrender every day in all areas of life.

Father, may my life always be in tune with Your song.
May my life be an anthem of praise to You!

Yielding to God's Perfect Will

SURRENDERED TO GOD – JOURNAL DAY 28

Am I living in tune with God's Word or off-key in some area? How does my obedience praise Him?

_____

_____

_____

_____

_____

_____

_____

_____

SURRENDERED TO GOD - DAY 29

Surrendering to a Light Burden
(Matthew 11:30)

The Christian life requires *surrender* to the Lordship of Christ. Yet many people struggle with that term as they associate it with negative perceptions such as acknowledging defeat, giving up possession of something valuable, abandoning rights to something personal, or giving up control. From the perspective of these associations, the Lordship of Christ may appear to be burdensome and personally threatening. But in the context of a loving God who is all-knowing and has the best interests of His children at heart, His yoke is easy, and His burden is light (Matthew 11:30). May we be wise enough to join Him, surrender to Him, and become a small part of the great things He has in store for us in this world and the world to come.

Faithful Father, You know all things and hold them in Your powerful hands. I love You, trust You, and joyfully want to contribute to Your kingdom.

SURRENDERED TO GOD - JOURNAL DAY 29

How does acknowledging God's loving, sovereign control encourage me to surrender fully to Him?

_____

_____

_____

_____

_____

_____

_____

_____

_____

SURRENDERED TO GOD – DAY 30

Fear Not and Remain Humble
(Isaiah 41:10; James 4:10)

"Fear not…for I *am* your God." "Humble yourselves in the sight of the Lord." Resistance to obey or follow God's leading usually stems from fear or pride. Fear, the opposite of faith, usually comes from perceived failure, humiliation, or rejection. The driving forces behind pride include not getting the expected results, a perceived image loss, relinquishing control, or fear of failure. Yet, neither fear nor pride are qualities God desires. He hates pride (Proverbs 6:17) and repeatedly reassures us to "Fear not." To build our faith, He consistently encourages us to trust completely (John 14:1), live courageously (2 Timothy 1:7), and love fearlessly (1 John 4:18). Additionally, He promises to strengthen, help, and uphold us with His righteous hand (Isaiah 41:10).

Father, help me to be bold in faith, fearless in love, and humble in obedience.

Yielding to God's Perfect Will

SURRENDERED TO GOD - JOURNAL DAY 30

How has this 30-day journey encouraged me to surrender fully to God? What are my next steps?

_____

_____

_____

_____

_____

_____

_____

_____

_____

SURRENDERED TO GOD – BONUS DAY

Ongoing Surrender and Transformation
(Luke 6:40)

"The disciple is not above his master: but every one that is perfect shall be as his master" (Luke 6:40, KJV). The master-servant, teacher-student, Jesus-follower relationship is plain here. The subordinate is not above his or her superior. The disciple takes up his cross, dies to self, and follows [obeys, imitates, or becomes like] Christ. The word *perfect* implies becoming complete or putting something in its appropriate position. The grammatical tense behind *every one that is perfect* implies a completed action with continuing results. As I follow, surrender to, and obey Jesus, I am becoming more like Him through His sanctifying Word and His transforming Spirit.

Jesus, I choose to follow and surrender to You. Please continue sanctifying and transforming me more and more into Your likeness.

Yielding to God's Perfect Will

SURRENDERED TO GOD – BONUS DAY

How am I becoming more like Jesus? What evidence of this transformation do I see in my life?

_____

_____

_____

_____

_____

_____

_____

_____

_____

ABOUT THE AUTHOR

A lifelong student of Scripture, Nate Stevens has also enjoyed a banking career in a variety of leadership roles. He is the author of *Matched 4 Life, Deck Time with Jesus, Transformed: Until Christ is Formed in You, Conformed: Into the Likeness of Christ, Informed: Living by God's Absolute Truth, God's Secret Place,* and *Accelerate Your Destiny* as well as a contributing author on several of the *Moments* Books *(Billy Graham Moments, Romantic Moments, Divine Moments, Spoken Moments, Christmas Moments, Stupid Moments, and Broken Moments).* He writes online articles for ChristianDevotions.us and KingdomWinds.com as well as several other ministries. He co-founded and leads Fusion, a Christian singles ministry. A popular speaker and teacher at conferences, seminars, and Bible study groups, he speaks on a wide variety of topics. Nate has two adult children. He and his wife, Karen, live near Charlotte, North Carolina.

Follow Nate and find more resources at:
www.natestevens.net

www.ingramcontent.com/pod-product-compliance
Lightning Source LLC
Chambersburg PA
CBHW071254070526
44583CB00017B/2458